VOL. 1

HAL•LEONARD®

TRUMPET
PLAY-ALONG

AUDIO
ACCESS
INCLUDED

POPULAR HITS

CONTENTS

2	Copacabana (At the Copa)	BARRY MANIOW
6	Does Anybody Really Know What Time It Is?	CHICAGO
36	Hot Hot Hot	BUSTER POINDEXTER
10	Livin' La Vida Loca	RICKY MARTIN
16	Ring of Fire	JOHNNY CASH
20	Sir Duke	STEVIE WONDER
24	Sussudio	PHIL COLLINS
32	Will It Go Round in Circles	BILLY PRESTON

To access audio visit:
www.halleonard.com/mylibrary

Enter Code
4564-0723-7649-0924

ISBN 978-1-4950-0011-9

Visit Hal Leonard Online at
www.halleonard.com

HAL•LEONARD®
CORPORATION
7777 W. BLUEMOUND RD. P.O. BOX 13819
MILWAUKEE, WISCONSIN 53213

Copacabana
(At the Copa)

from Barry Manilow's COPACABANA
Music by Barry Manilow
Lyric by Bruce Sussman and Jack Feldman

Her name was Lo - la; ___ she was a
Ri - co; ___ he wore a
Lo - la; ___ she was a

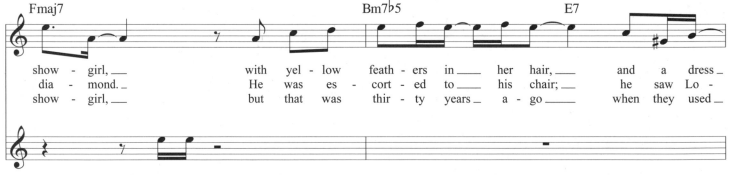

show - girl, ___ with yel - low feath - ers in ___ her hair, ___ and a dress ___
dia - mond. ___ He was es - cort - ed to ___ his chair; ___ he saw Lo -
show - girl, ___ but that was thir - ty years ___ a - go ___ when they used ___

___ cut down ___ to there. ___ She would me - ren - gue ___ and do the
- la danc - ing there, and when she fin - ished, ___ he called her
___ to have ___ a show. Now it's a dis - co, ___ but not for

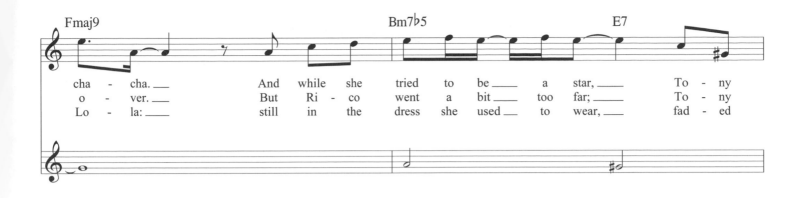

cha - cha. ____ And while she tried to be ____ a star, ____ To - ny
o - ver. ____ But Ri - co went a bit ____ too far; ____ To - ny
Lo - la: ____ still in the dress she used ___ to wear, ____ fad - ed

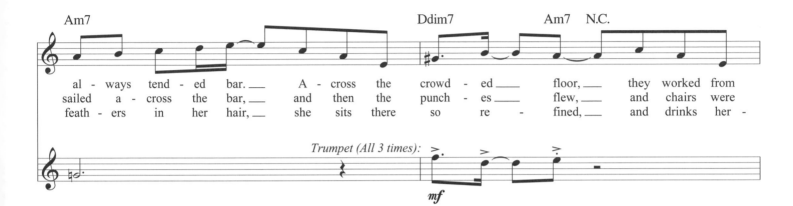

al - ways tend - ed bar. ____ A - cross the crowd - ed ____ floor, ____ they worked from
sailed a - cross the bar, ____ and then the punch - es ____ flew, ____ and chairs were
feath - ers in her hair, ____ she sits there so re - fined, ____ and drinks her -

Trumpet (All 3 times):

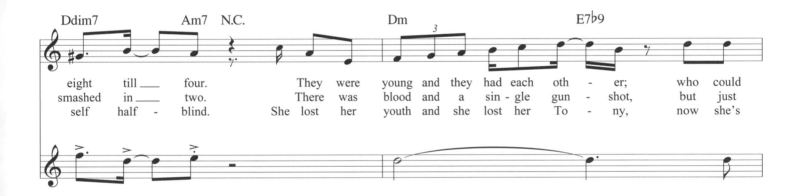

eight till ____ four. They were young and they had each oth - er; who could
smashed in ____ two. There was blood and a sin - gle gun - shot, but just
self half - blind. She lost her youth and she lost her To - ny, now she's

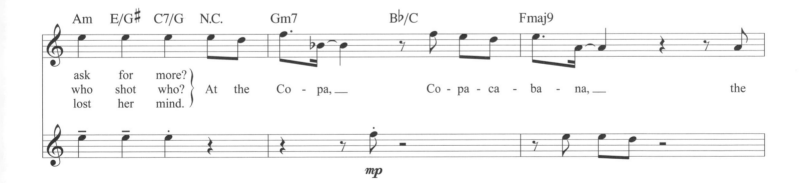

ask for more? }
who shot who? } At the Co - pa, ____ Co - pa - ca - ba - na, ____ the
lost her mind. }

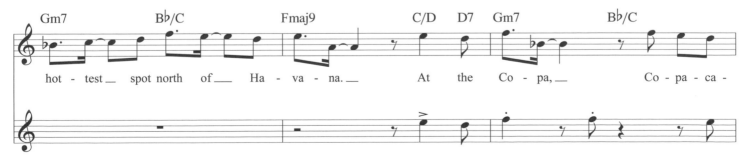

hot - test ____ spot north of ____ Ha - va - na. ____ At the Co - pa, ____ Co - pa - ca -

ba - na. __ Mu - sic __ and pas - sion __ were al - ways __ the fash - ion at the

Co - pa. __ They fell in love.

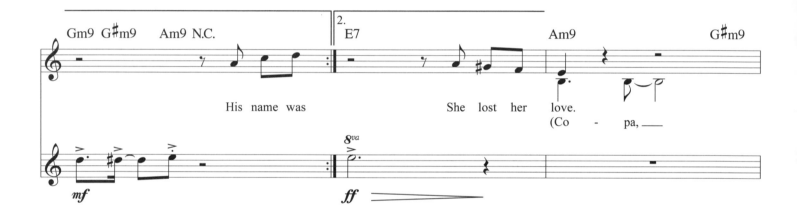

His name was She lost her love. (Co - pa, __

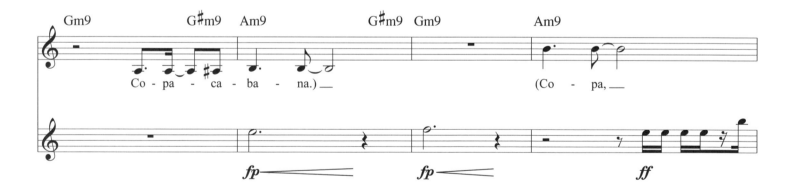

Co - pa - ca - ba - na.) __ (Co - pa, __

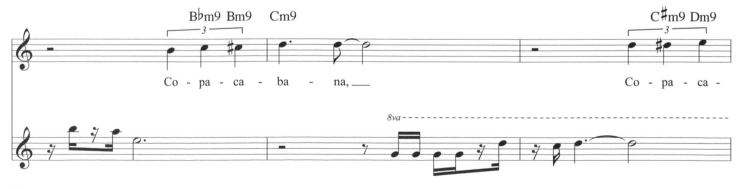

Co - pa - ca - ba - na, __ Co - pa - ca -

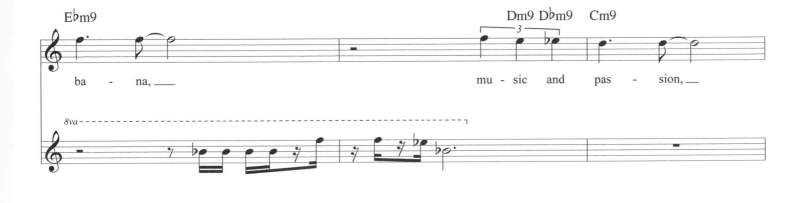

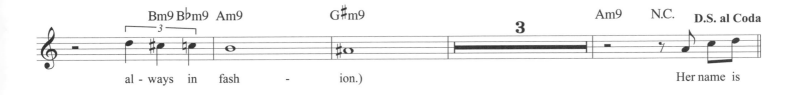

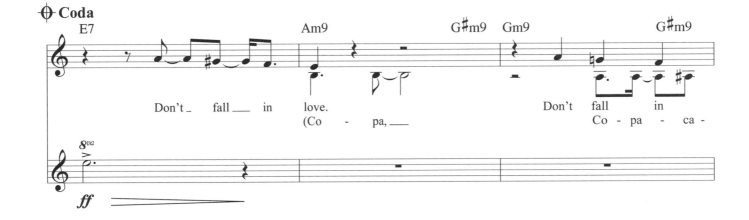

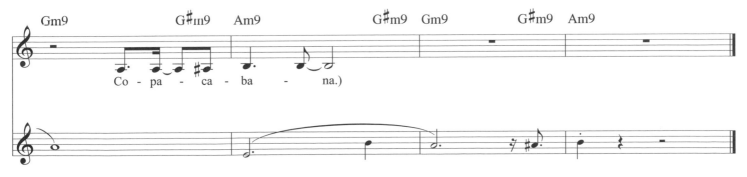

Does Anybody Really Know What Time It Is?

Words and Music by Robert Lamm

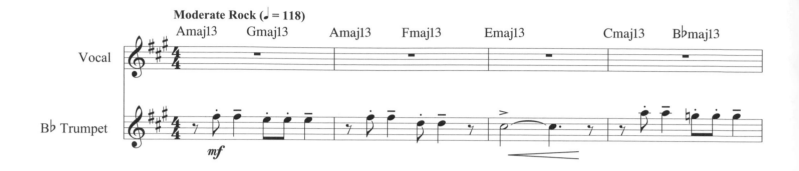

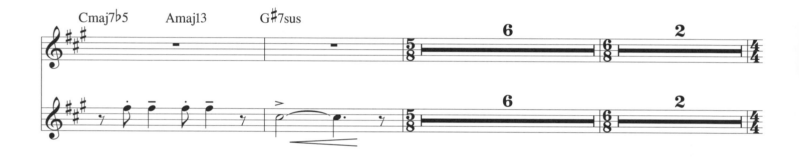

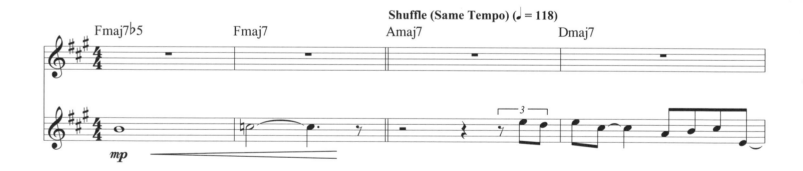

1. As I was walk-
2. When I was walk-
3. *(See additional lyrics)*

- ing down __ the street __ one day, __   a man __
- ing down __ the street __ one day, __   a pret-

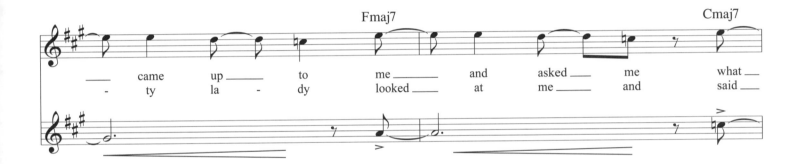

__ came up __ to me __ and asked __ me what __
- ty la - dy looked __ at me __ and said __

__ the time __ was that __ was on __ my watch, _____ yeah, __
__ her dia - mond watch __ had stopped cold dead, _____

and I said, _____ }
and I said, _____ }

7

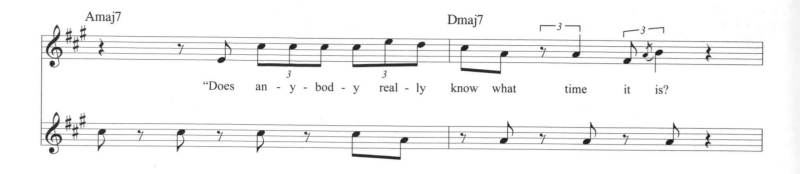

"Does an-y-bod-y really know what time it is?

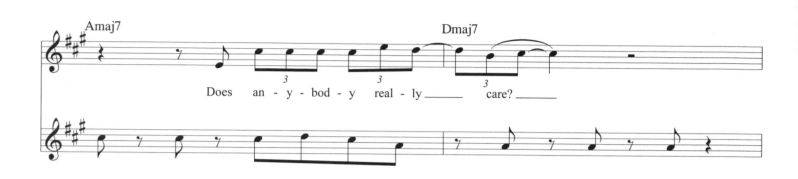

Does an-y-bod-y really ____ care? ____

If so, I can't im-ag-ine why ____ we've all got time

1., 2.
e-nough to cry. ____

3.
e-nough to die. ____

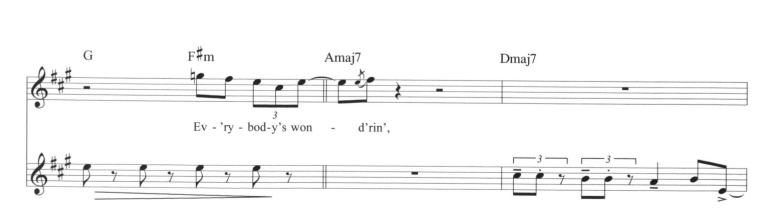

Ev-'ry-bod-y's won ____ d'rin',

and I don't care,_____ well, a-bout time,

I don't care._____

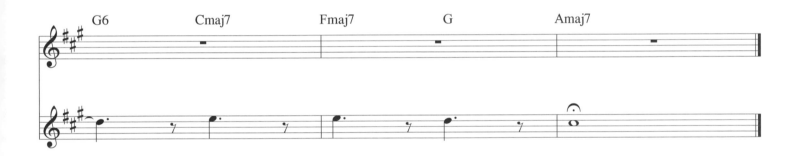

Additional Lyrics

And I was walking down the street one day,
Being pushed and shoved by people trying to
Beat the clock, oh, oh, I just don't know,
I don't know, I don't know.
And I said, yes I said,
Chorus

Livin' La Vida Loca

Words and Music by Desmond Child and Robi Rosa

new ad - dic - tions _____ for ev - 'ry day and night. _ (1., D.S.) She'll
took my mon - ey. _____ She must -'ve slipped me a sleep - ing pill. _ (2.) She

G#m
make you take _ your clothes _ off and _ go danc - ing in _ the rain. _
nev - er drinks _ the wa - ter, makes you or - der French cham - pagne. _

A#m

B
___ She'll make _____ you live _ her cra - zy life. _ Well, she'll take
Once you've had _ a taste _ of her, _ you'll _ nev -

C#
___ a - way _ your pain _____ like a bul - let to your brain. _ *(Come on!)*
- er be _ the same. _ Yeah, she'll make _ you go in - sane. _ *(Oh, boy!)*

A#   To Coda ⊕

D#m
Out - side _ in - side out, _ she's liv - in' la vi - da _ lo -

C#

D.S. al Coda
(Verse 1)

CODA

She'll

D#m

Out - side __ in - side out, __ she's

f

C#

liv - in' la vi - da __ lo - ca. __ She'll push and __ pull __

D#m

___ you down, liv - in' la vi - da __ lo - ca. Her

C#

D#m

lips are ___ dev - il ___ red, ___ and her skin's the col - or of mo-

- cha. She will ___ wear ___ you ___ out, ___

1.
D♯m

2.
D♯m

liv - in' la vi - da ___ lo - ca. - ca.

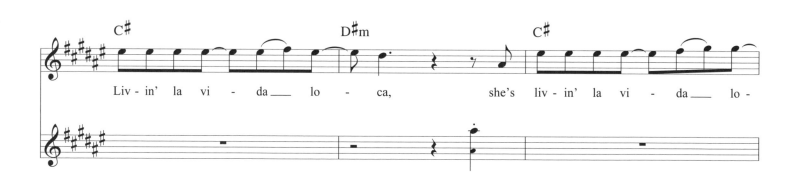

Liv - in' la vi - da ___ lo - ca, she's liv - in' la vi - da ___ lo-

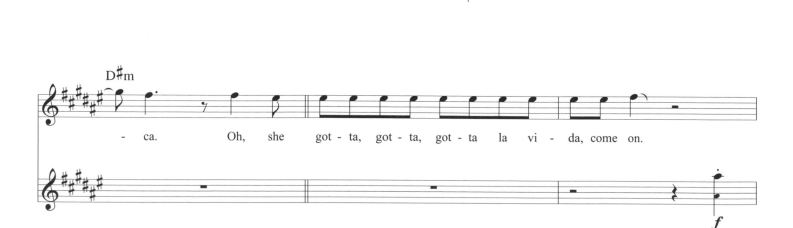

- ca. Oh, she got - ta, got - ta, got - ta la vi - da, come on.

f

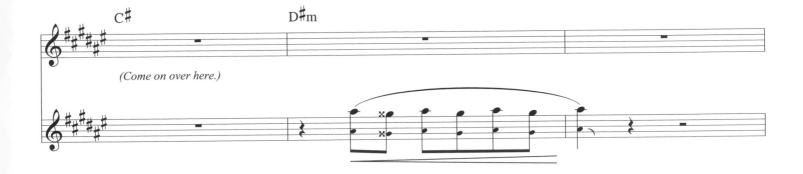

(Come on over here.)

Solo:

Come on!

Got - ta la vi - da lo - ca,   I

got - ta, got - ta, got - ta la vi - da lo - ca,   got - ta, got - ta, got - ta la vi....

Ring of Fire

Words and Music by Merle Kilgore and June Carter

Sir Duke

Words and Music by Stevie Wonder

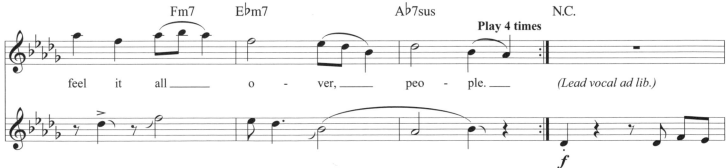

Db

1.,2. You   can
3.–6. *Lead vocal ad lib.*

f

Gm   Gbmaj7

feel   it   all _____   o - ver, _____   you   can

Fm7   Ebm7   Ab7sus   **Play 6 times**   N.C.

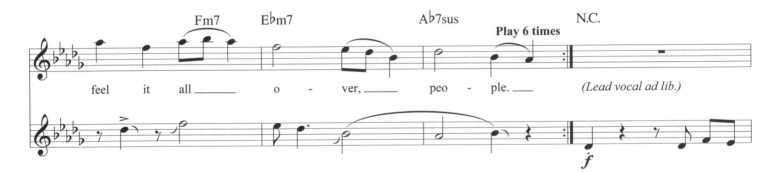

feel   it   all _____   o - ver, _____   peo - ple. _____   *(Lead vocal ad lib.)*

ff

Sussudio
Words and Music by Phil Collins

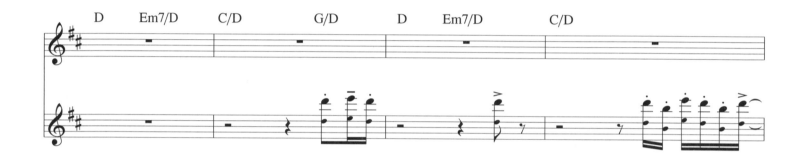

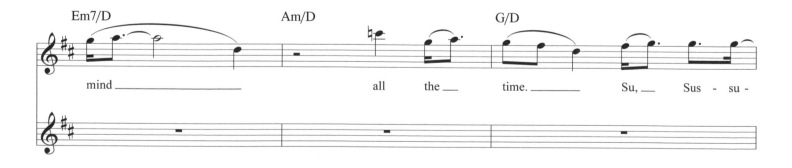

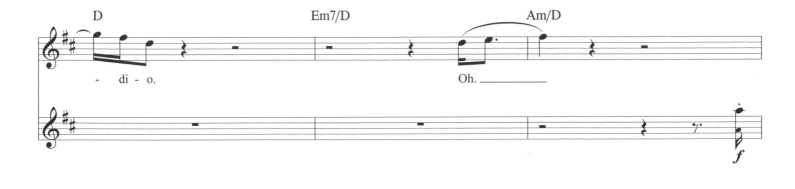

-di - o.　　Oh.____

Now,　she don't e - ven know　my __　name,____　but I

think she likes me just __ the __ same.____　Su, Sus - su - di - o.____

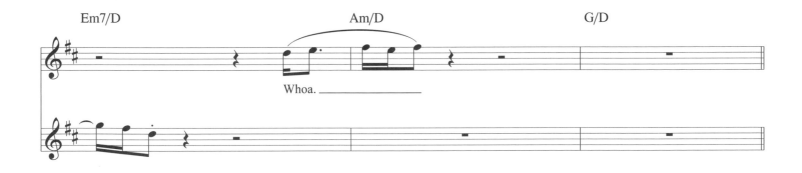

Whoa.____

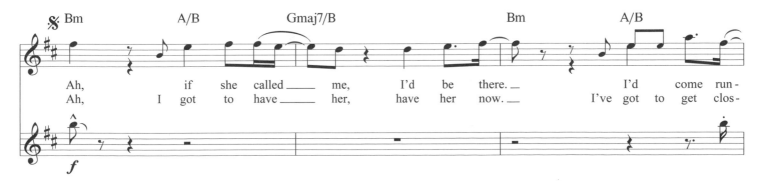

Ah,　　　if she called ____ me,　I'd　be　there.__　　I'd　come run -
Ah,　I　got　to have ____ her,　have　her　now.__　I've　got　to　get　clos -

-nin' an - y - where. _____ She's all I need, all my life.
-er, but I don't _ know how. _____ She makes me ner - vous, it makes me scared.

I feel so _ good, _ if I just say the word, _____

_____ Su, Sus - su - di - o. Just say the

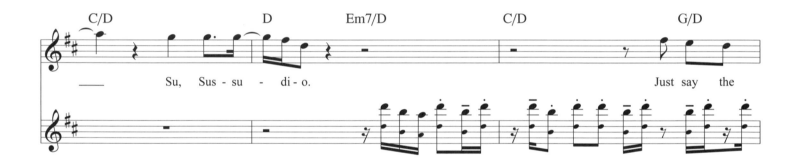

word, oh, _____ Su, Sus - su - di - o. _____
(Lead vocal ad lib. on D.S.)

Now, I know that I'm too _ young. _____

My life has just __ be - gun. _____ Su, Sus - su - di - o.

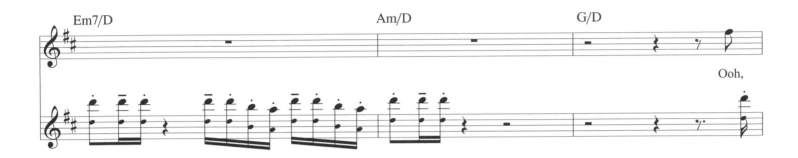

Ooh,

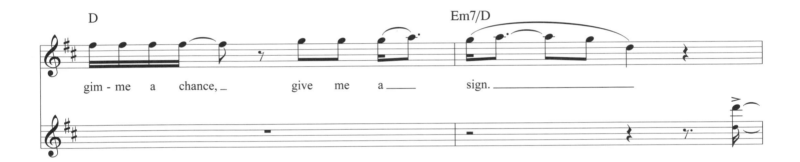

gim - me a chance, __ give me a __ sign. _____

I'd show her an - y - time. _____ Su, Su, __ Sus - su - di - o. _____

D.S. al Coda

Oh. _____

CODA

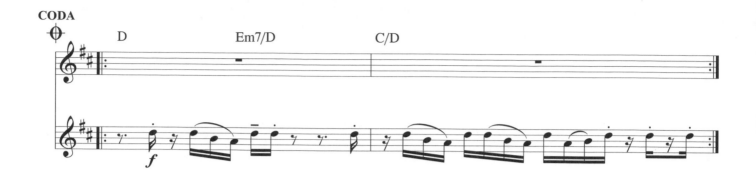

Ah, she's all I need, _ all my life. I feel so _ good, _

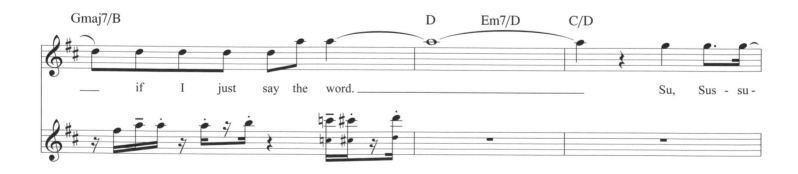

_ if I just say the word. _____ Su, Sus - su -

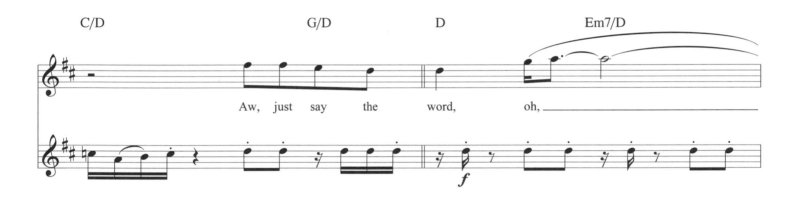

Will It Go Round In Circles

Words and Music by Billy Preston and Bruce Fisher

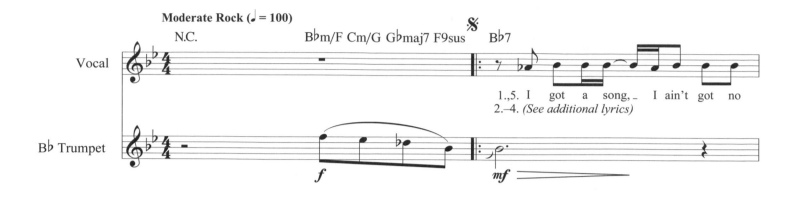

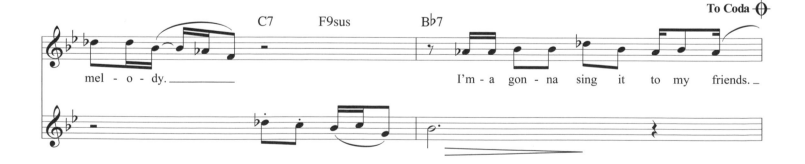

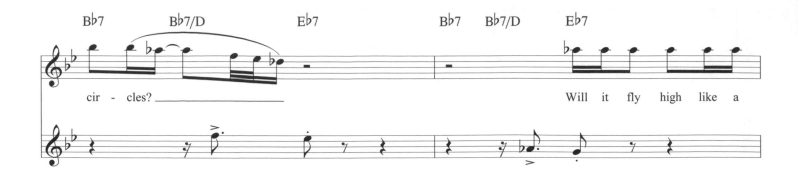

cir - cles? _____ Will it fly high like a

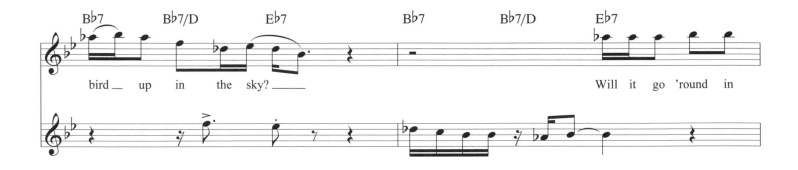

bird __ up in the sky? _____ Will it go 'round in

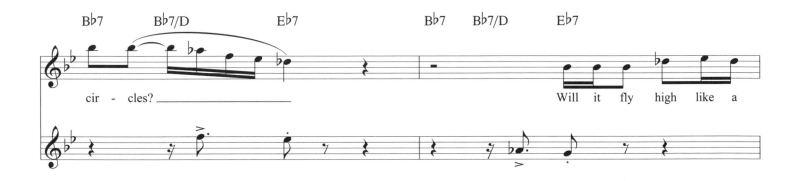

cir - cles? _____ Will it fly high like a

D.S. al Coda

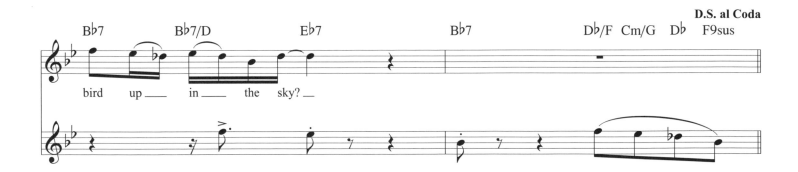

bird up __ in __ the sky? __

CODA

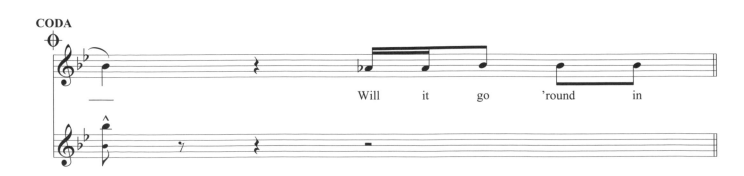

__ Will it go 'round in

cir - cles? _____

Will it fly high_ like a

bird up in the sky? _____

Will it go 'round in

cir - cles? _____

Will it fly high like a

Repeat and Fade

bird up _ in the sky? _

Ooh!

Additional Lyrics

2. I've got a story, ain't got no moral.
   Let the bad guy win ev'ry once in a while.
   I've got a story, ain't got no moral.
   Let the bad guy win ev'ry once in a while.
   Chorus

3. I've got a dance, ain't got no steps.
   I'm gonna let the music move me around.
   I've got a dance, ain't got no steps.
   I'm gonna let the music move me around.
   Chorus

4. *Instrumental*

Hot Hot Hot

Words and Music by Alphonsus Cassell

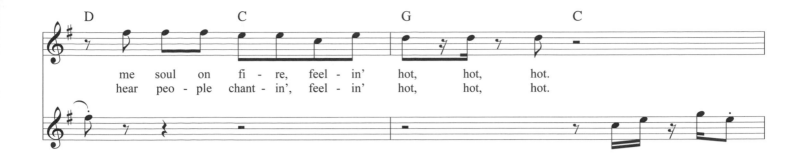

me soul on fi - re, feel - in' hot, hot, hot.
hear peo - ple chant - in', feel - in' hot, hot, hot.

Par - ty peo - ple
Keep up the spir - it,

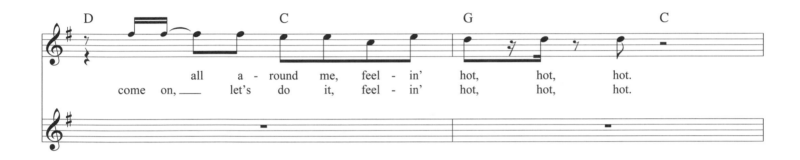

all a - round me, feel - in' hot, hot, hot.
come on, ___ let's do it, feel - in' hot, hot, hot.

Oh, what to do ___ on a night like
It's in the air, ___ cel - e - bra - tion

this, mu - sic sweet, I can't
time. Mu - sic sweet, cap - ti - vate your ___

Peo-ple in the par-ty, hot, hot, hot. They come to the par-ty, know what they got. They

come to the par-ty, know what they got. I'm hot, you're hot,

he's hot, she's hot. (Real hot, real hot.)

How you feel-in'? (Hot, hot, hot.)

How you feel-in'? (Hot, hot, hot.) (Hot, hot, hot.

Hot, hot, hot.) (Hot, hot, hot, hot. Hot, hot, hot.)
(Lead vocal ad lib.) (¿Como esta?)

G D7 G D7 G D7 **Repeat and Fade**

f *f*